ACKNOWLEDGEMENTS
Thanks to Tom Behan, Chris Harman, Carmela Ozzi
and Mark Thomas.

ABOUT THE AUTHOR
Chris Bambery is the editor of Socialist Worker and is a leading
member of the Socialist Workers Party (www.swp.org.uk)

INSIDE FRONT PHOTOGRAPH
Anti-fascists in Parma build barricades 1922.

INSIDE BACK PHOTOGRAPH
A picture of Gramsci is carried by a crowd in
Sardinia after the fall of fascism.

PUBLISHED BY BOOKMARKS PUBLICATIONS 2006
ISBN: 1905192150
DESIGNED BY NOEL DOUGLAS (noel@noeldouglas.net)

PRINTED BY CAMBRIDGE PRINTING

A Rebel's Guide to

GRAMSCI

CHRIS BAMBERY

★ 1:
AN
ITALIAN
OUTSIDER

Antonio Gramsci was born in Italy, a country that was just three decades old at the time of his birth. This new state was riven by a number of critical fault lines.

His evolution as a Marxist was profoundly influenced by his birthplace and then by the city where he grew to political maturity.

He was born on the island of Sardinia in 1891. It was physically separate from "continental" Italy but was very much part of the Italian south. The south had been the great loser in the process that had unified most of present-day Italy by 1861. As elsewhere in the south, poverty, famine, disease and illiteracy dominated Sardinia. Elections were fixed by local landlords. Gramsci's family were middle class, but they had fallen on hard times. When Gramsci's father crossed the local political boss he was jailed on false charges.

But new forces were at work on the island. Its miners were influenced by socialist ideas and took part in a strike. The owners found this was a revolt that was not so easy to repress. Antonio's brother was conscripted into the army, and while serving in Turin he began reading socialist papers that he sent home to his younger brother. Gramsci's anger against the conditions dominating the island meant that he turned to Sardinian nationalism, which blamed the "continentals" in Rome and Milan for the island's ills.

After finishing his schooling, which had been interrupted by the need to work and illness which left him permanently disabled and sickly, Gramsci moved to the northern city that forged him into a revolutionary Marxist — Turin. He won a scholarship to the city's university, where he began studying in 1911. The young Antonio Gramsci arriving in that city carried his anger against "continentals" with him. But in Turin he discovered something that had a dramatic impact on his life and to whose importance he returned to as a reference point again and again — Turin was home to one of the most combative working classes of all times.

★ 2: TURIN: A STORM CENTRE OF REVOLUTION

Turin in the early years of the 20th century was experiencing a rapid industrialisation similar to that of many Chinese and Indian cities today. It was a city dominated by the new car industry and by the huge FIAT company in particular. Turin's population by the time Gramsci arrived was 400,000, with 20 percent industrial workers.

The Italian Socialist Party (PSI) and the Italian trade union movement were both still in their infancy. The former was still largely dominated by middle class professionals who wanted to improve the lives of the lower orders and rejected revolution. The unions tended to look to skilled workers only and the main trade union federation, the CGL, was closely allied to the Socialist Party's moderate leaders.

Both groups had accepted an agreement with Giovanni Giolitti, who led a succession of coalition governments in the first two decades of the 20th century, wheeling and dealing between the various local interests that dominated Italian politics. He hoped to incorporate the socialist and trade union leaders.

The rank and file of Turin's socialists attempted to secure the nomination to parliament of a radical figure from the south who had highlighted injustice there. The attempt failed, but Gramsci was drawn in and began to see that northern workers were the allies of southern peasants and labourers and that a socialist revolution was the only way to bring real change to the south.

By then Gramsci, a gifted student who shone academically despite poverty and illness, had met a talented group of young socialists at Turin University. His arrival in the city corresponded with mounting social conflict. Across Europe the ideas of liberalism that had dominated established politics were giving way to a more aggressive sort of ruling class politics. Competition between the great powers was intensifying. Abroad this meant trying to grab ever more chunks of the globe. At home it meant growing pressure to hold down wages and to boost productivity. The failed Russian Revolution of 1905 further encouraged Europe's rulers to crack down on the left and labour unrest.

In Italy industrialists and landlords demanded that, rather than negotiate with the unions and the left, the government should use the full weight of the state against them. Many wanted Italy to conquer colonies in Africa so it could emulate France and Britain.

In 1911 Turin engineering workers rose up in an unofficial general strike against attacks on working conditions that union leaders had agreed to. The strike was defeated after 75 days. But in the following year in order to recoup support the engineering union (FIOM) led a 93 day strike. A new feature was the creation from below of rank and file bodies, called internal commissions, elected on the factory floor by all workers, regardless of whether they held a union card. Outside of a strike situation the union leadership tried to absorb and neuter these bodies but their existence meant they could be revived when necessary.

On both sides of the class divide attitudes were hardening. In 1911 Giolitti tried to appease his critics by launching an expedition to colonise what is now Libya. Inside the PSI a younger generation demanded a break with the accord with Giolitti. It found expression in their growing support for southern peasants and labourers, who were subject to merciless repression whenever they protested, and in a rising mood of opposition to militarism and colonialism. The Sardinian Gramsci already sympathised with colonial rebellions against the European powers and regarded the "Southern Question" as key. All of this sharpened his interest in Marxism. In 1913 he was recruited to the Socialist Party by a fellow student, Angelo Tasca.

The magnet for the discontent with the cautious, collaborationist leaders of the PSI was a firebrand from the rebellious Romagna region, Benito Mussolini. After opposing Italy's imperialist conquest of Libya and a barnstorming speech at a party congress attacking the temporising right wing of the PSI, Mussolini won the editorship of the party's daily paper, Avanti ("Forward").

★3:
SOCIALISM
ITALIAN
STYLE

Italy's Socialist Party was polarising between a reformist right wing minority who were eager to join a government, almost any government, and the rank and file who voted the left into control. The left led by Giacinto Serrati espoused, loudly and verbosely, the party's maximum programme of revolution: thus they were termed "maximalists". The reformists stressed the party's minimum programme of immediate reforms. What was missing was any attempt at bridging a fight in the here and now and the longer term task of revolution.

In June 1914 a demonstration against the shipping of troops to Albania (which Italy had effectively colonised) grew into an insurrection which spread across the Romagna region. Whole towns were taken over and socialist republics declared as the red flag was run up on the town halls. Both the PSI and the unions failed to act and the rising was suppressed by the army.

As the war clouds gathered across Europe, Mussolini's calls from his newspaper desk for a general strike against war and for revolution grew louder. The truth was that there was little substance to all this beyond a demand for action. But that was music to the ears of Gramsci and many young socialists.

In August 1914 tension between the European

powers erupted into war. Italy had entered into an alliance with Germany and Austria, hoping this would gain it territories in the Balkans and along its Alpine border. Now it refused to go to war in honour of that alliance and began touting itself round the European capitals seeking the best rewards for entering the growing bloodbath.

Inside the country the nationalist right demanded the government declare war on the side of France and Britain (Austria had been the historic enemy of Italian unification). Sections of big business were eyeing the lucrative contracts war would bring, Giolitti's rivals wanted him out and all, including the king and a ragbag of poets and artists, wanted an empire.

By May 1915, aided by French and British subsidies, the right were demanding war. The king and Giolitti's replacement as premier wanted war, having signed a secret treaty with Britain and France whereby Italy would gain territories across the Balkans, the Middle East and North Africa (the Bolsheviks would publish this and much else after the 1917 Russian Revolution).

Italy was divided. Giolitti supported neutrality, believing Italy could profit more. The powerful Catholic church opposed war as it could not side with one Catholic country against another without damaging its interests and wealth. The PSI stood out among Western European socialist parties in opposing war, but only on the basis of supporting neutrality and opposing any active opposition to the war effort.

As parliament hesitated about voting for war, the right took to the streets. A little pressure was sufficient to swing the vote. On the right a myth was created of a nation united apart from the left extremists and priests whose loyalty to the pope surpassed that to Italy. More importantly, the right had tasted victory through using extra-parliamentary action (albeit protests aided and abetted by the police and army and funded by big business). In Turin a general strike took place against war but the city was left to fight alone, not for the first or last time, and it was suppressed.

But what of the firebrand and anti-militarist Mussolini? In the autumn of 1914 he suddenly declared his opposition to neutrality. It was a short step to endorsing Italy's entry into the war. Jumping before he was pushed Mussolini quit the PSI to launch a new paper, Il Popolo d'Italia ("The Italian People"). It was funded by arms manufacturers and Anglo-French handouts. After a short service in the army (he was invalided out after an accident with a grenade) he returned to his newspaper desk in Milan.

Mussolini's defection was a bombshell. Small numbers of union activists, PSI members and anarchists decamped with him but his young supporters in the socialist party were shell-shocked. In Turin Gramsci wrote a poor article trying to explain Mussolini's initial step of rejecting neutrality and then collapsed into a nervous breakdown.

★4:
THE
TEST
OF
WAR

The war was a disaster for Italy. Peasant conscripts (industrial workers were needed in the factories) were herded into a series of futile frontal attacks on Austro-German positions in the frozen Alps by one of the most bone-headed, corrupt and privileged officer corps in Europe (and there was much competition). Industrialists made vast profits — some, like the tyre manufacturer Pirelli, by selling material to Germany via neutral Switzerland.

Turin swelled further in size, drawing in workers from its rural surrounds and also huge numbers of women. These soon chafed at increased work discipline and the erosion of wages as prices soared. As elsewhere in Europe skilled engineers became more militant as privileges they had won were eroded by mechanisation.

In October of 1917 a German-Austrian offensive broke through at Caporetto — 300,000 Italian troops surrendered and a similar number deserted, often after their officers had left the front. The routed Italian army fell back nearly to Venice and threatened Italy's total defeat. In an attempt to rally the troops the government promised conscripts that land would be given to them after the war.

The aftermath of Caporetto also saw a policy of breakneck industrial expansion. Italy would end the war with more artillery than Britain and as an exporter of trucks and aircraft to its allies. By the end of the war there were half a million engineering workers and the trade unions swelled in size to 3 million. Yet inflation undermined working class living standards and matters were made worse by serious food shortages as Italian agriculture could not feed the new industrial centres. The factories were put under military discipline with hours of work increased and strikes outlawed.

★5:
WAR
AGAINST
WAR

The Russian Revolution found more of an echo in Turin than in any other Western European city. News of the first revolution in Russia, which had toppled the Tsar in February 1917, electrified the city and there was widespread hope that it would be followed by a second, workers' revolution that would remove Russia from the war.

A delegation from Russia arrived in Turin on 15 August 1917 to address a mass rally of munitions workers. The Russians were all supporters of continuing the war and wanted to urge their Italian brothers and sisters to help them by producing more weapons of mass destruction. To their utter amazement they were greeted with repeated cries of "Viva Lenin!"

On 21 August 1917 eight bakeries in the city failed to open. Women and children began demonstrating to demand bread across the city. The authorities rushed in flour but the protests were already moving on to the political plane. A worker at the Diatto-Frejus plant recalled that "instead of entering the factory, we began a demonstration outside the gates, shouting, 'We haven't eaten. We can't work. We want bread!'" The factory owner assured the crowd that bread was coming: "The workers were quiet for a moment. They looked at each other as though they were tacitly conferring. Then they all together shouted, 'To hell with the bread! We want peace! Down with the profiteers! Down with the War!' And they left the factory en masse" (John M Cammett, Antonio Gramsci and the Origins of Italian Communism, Stanford University Press, 1967, p52).

Clashes began between workers and police, and then soldiers. Barricades went up in working class areas. Several army barracks were attacked and two churches set ablaze (reflecting popular attitudes towards the church). Eventually the workers were driven back by tanks and machine guns. Fifty workers died and others were sent to military tribunals or directly to frontline units in the trenches.

Two reasons underlay the failure of the insurrection. Firstly, despite all the revolutionary declarations of the PSI leaders there was no plan of action and little or no coordination. Turin had been left to fight and to face defeat alone. Secondly, there were reports of isolated army units throwing down their weapons but the workers failed to win over the troops. The decisive unit involved in repressing them was a Sardinian brigade. This gave added spice to Gramsci's insistence on unity between northern workers and southern peasants.

The Socialist Party in the city, firmly on the left of the party, brought militants from the factories together with community activists and all were subjected to the influence of the debates swirling around the party and the international movement.

Nationally the anti-war section of the Socialist Party responded to the rising in Turin by calling a meeting in Florence that November. Before it was broken up by the police it heard a young Neapolitan revolutionary, Amadeo Bordiga, tell the meeting that the time for action was now and that they must act. Italy was not yet ready for insurrection but hot on the news from Petrograd (now St Petersburg) of the October Revolution, it caught the mood of young socialists in the hall like Gramsci.

The war had created a cocktail of unrest. In Turin the strike against Italy's entry into the war, the 1917 bread riots and the surge of self-organisation in the factories created the potential for economic and political demands to fuse. Meanwhile, the peasant conscripts returned from the trenches burning with a sense of injustice and "contaminated" with new ideas from the cities of the north. They bitterly discovered that the promises of land had been lies.

The old order on the land was fast eroding. As early as 1915 peasants had already begun seizing land in the Lazio region — the example began to spread across Italy. The word was spreading among peasants and landless labourers that in Russia the revolution had given the land to the people.

Peasants and landless labourers had made up the majority of conscripts. In contrast the upper classes ensured their sons avoided frontline service. One wartime prime minister, Salandra, had three sons of the required age who somehow were never called up.

★6: THE HOME FRONT

In this situation workers began to create their own rank and file organisations of resistance. The internal commissions began to revive and would re-emerge in full cry after the First World War. Assemblies gathered to discuss pay and conditions involving all those in a section or plant. This had added importance because there had been a surge of women and other new workers into the factories who had little or no tradition of union membership.

Naturally union officials disliked such bodies because they involved non-union members and pre-vented the officials from acting as mediators between the shopfloor, the management and the military. In April 1918 the engineering union, FIOM, won an agreement raising wages, guaranteeing unemployment insurance and recognising the internal commissions. The downside was that once more the union moved to co-opt and dis-cipline these bodies.

The Italian ruling class was divided. Italy had failed to garner all of the bribes proffered to it when it entered the war. The peace treaties which followed the war left a section of the ruling class and a swathe of the middle class, particularly former and serving officers, seething.

The established politicians might protest but could

see no other alternative but to accept the reduced territorial gains offered. A nationalist poet and war hero, Gabriele d'Annunzio, led a paramilitary takeover of the city of Fiume which had been incorporated into the new Balkan state of Yugoslavia. The military aided and abetted this adventure. This gave added impetus to the right to look to extra-parliamentary means to achieve their aims. The government in Rome was being ignored by growing numbers of the population, both on the left and on the right.

In no other Western European country did the conditions approximate to Russia as much as they did in Italy. The Italian royal family believed the fate of their Romanov relatives in Russia awaited them. The army command feared it could not rely on its own men. A combination of rural and urban rebellion looked set to sweep all of them away. Italy was entering a revolutionary crisis, the "biennio rosso", the two red years of 1919 and 1920.

★7: THE FACTORY COUNCILS

Gramsci was looking for the means whereby a future socialist society could cease to be an abstraction. The factory councils represented a potential bridge into the future.

In Turin in 1919 and 1920 workers came together in their factories to elect new organisations, factory councils (or internal committees as they were also known), directly elected on the shopfloor. These went beyond trade unions in organising all workers regardless of whether they belonged to a union or not. In the trade unions workers were individual members, often separated from fellow workers who were in different unions and they were concerned largely with wages and conditions.

Gramsci, of course, believed workers should be in the unions, but he saw that the factory councils went further, allowing them to join together as a collective to run the plant. "The Council realises in practice the unity of the working class; it gives the masses the same form and cohesion they adopt in the general organisation of society" (Gramsci, Selections from Political Writings 1910-1920, p100).

These factory councils took on a revolutionary dynamic when they began to challenge management's right to control the very process of production. They could be the basis on which to build a new workers' state.

The basis for a new unity in the workplace was also being laid. In March 1919 white collar staff in Turin's engineering plants went on strike over regrading. Many blue collar workers were laid off during a long strike but they maintained solidarity with a group who traditionally had stood aside from militancy and had regarded themselves as a cut above manual workers. The idea that blue and white collar workers should be united gathered pace and fed into idea that permanent factory-wide organisation was a necessity.

The new councils were elected by all, regardless of their political or religious ideas, regardless of party affiliation and whether they carried a trade union membership card. These councils had the potential to draw in all who helped produce — technicians and white collar workers, who regarded themselves in those days as middle class, together with peasants and rural labourers. These people would stop being nameless cogs in the production process and assert their own identity and power.

Gramsci, unlike the maximalists or Bordiga, who led the opposition to them from the left, was trying to address how the working class could move forward from the present to the future. He insisted, "The socialist state already exists potentially in the institutions of social life characteristic of the exploited working class." He went on to explain that "the internal commissions are organs of workers' democracy which must be freed from the limitations imposed on them by the entrepreneurs, and infused with new life and energy. Today the internal commissions limit the power of the capitalist in the factory... Tomorrow, developed, and enriched, they must be organs of proletarian power, replacing the capitalist in all his useful functions of management and administration" (Gramsci, SPW 1910-20, pp65-66).

Gramsci urged the workers to call mass assemblies in the factories to elect delegates under the slogan "All power in the workshop to the workshop committees", together with its complement, "All state power to the workers' and peasants' councils".

Prior to 1917 the tradition on the left was to operate in two separate spheres — as a good workplace activist during working hours and in the evenings and weekends as a socialist spreading the word and waging election campaigns.

What was missing was a method to link day to day battles in the factories with the fight for the socialist future. Gramsci saw the factory councils as uniting the two, bridging the gap capitalist society insists on between political and economic demands. Gramsci believed that the factory councils could act to revolutionise the unions and the Italian Socialist Party.

The creation of rank and file councils was happening to a greater or lesser extent in centres of industry stretching from Petrograd in Russia, through Budapest in Hungary and Berlin in Germany to Glasgow on the far away Clyde. It was the factory councils, from which the Russian soviets sprang, which had voted to seize power in October 1917, representing as they did millions of workers, peasants and soldiers.

★ 8: THE NEW ORDER

The stress on creating councils of workers' power became the central message of a weekly political review, L'Ordine Nuovo ("The New Order"), which Gramsci launched together with a group of friends in May 1919. It would win itself a popular audience in the factories of Turin. As a guide for the paper Gramsci borrowed the maxim of the French writer Romain Rolland, "Pessimism of the intellect, optimism of the will."

L'Ordine Nuovo campaigned for all workers to be given the right to vote for the factory councils and for each section in a workplace to elect their own representative, to deepen rank and file control and involvement.

Looking back in August 1920 Gramsci recalled that "the problem of the development of the internal commission became the central problem, the idea, of L'Ordine Nuovo. It came to be seen as the fundamental problem of the workers' revolution... L'Ordine Nuovo became the 'journal of the factory councils'. The workers loved L'Ordine Nuovo (this we can state with inner satisfaction) and why did they love it? Because in its articles they rediscovered a part, the best part, of themselves... Because its articles were virtually a 'taking note' of actual events, seen as moments of a process of inner liberation and self-expression on the part of the working class. This is why the workers loved L'Ordine Nuovo and how its idea came to be 'formed'" (SPW 1910-1920, pp293-294).

Three crucial issues were emerging among the editors of L'Ordine Nuovo. One was the old argument that only those who held union membership could vote. The trade union leaders returned to this again and again and it would lead to a split on L'Ordine Nuovo between Tasca who sided with them, and Gramsci, who championed the new councils. Secondly, there was a tendency to see the new forms of control the factory councils exerted as co-existing alongside the old forms of management and private ownership. Again this was something the union leaders encouraged.

Gramsci and L'Ordine Nuovo tended to downplay the argument that workers' control could only be fully developed and maintained through a revolutionary change of society. But without that there was a tendency for the factory councils to be consumed in a plethora of individual disputes and to become no more than a new breed of admittedly more militant union representatives.

Thirdly, in emphasising the role of the factory councils as the means of creating workers' power Gramsci also downplayed the role of a revolutionary party to that of little more than a pressure group. In challenging the mechanical Marxism that saw the party as simply leading workers to the promised land he reacted too far. That meant he did not fight his corner inside the PSI, which left the field open to the maximalists and Bordiga, ensuring L'Ordine Nuovo and its supporters were isolated to Turin and its surrounding hinterland. Moreover the CGL and all the factions within the PSI were combined in wishing to isolate and defeat the "ordinovisti" (the supporters of L'Ordine Nuovo). Added to this the employers, awakened to the dangers of the contagion spreading out from Turin, were determined to break the factory councils.

★ 9: THE OCCUPATION OF THE FACTORIES

The decisive moment in the biennio rosso came in September 1920 when mass sackings of union members in Milan sparked factory occupations across Italy. By 4 September 400,000 workers were in occupied plants. Within a few days the number had reached 1 million. This occupation movement, while strongest in the north, swept the entire country. Finally, here was a truly national force to confront the capitalists and their state. These became more than occupations. In plant after plant the occupying workers restarted production under workers' control.

A jubilant Gramsci wrote, "One day like this is worth ten years of normal activity, normal propaganda and normal absorption of revolutionary notions and ideas" (Gramsci, SPW 1910-20, p340).

The occupations immediately reinvigorated the factory councils across Turin. At FIAT the council appointed special commissars to organise the security of the plant, to maintain transport and the supply of materials. Red Guards were also formed to protect the plants from possible attack. At the Spa plant hand grenades were made and distributed across the occupied factories, while one FIAT workshop specialised in making barbed wire.

Gramsci argued that Turin's factory councils should go further and create a citywide organisation and a military defence force, something that already existed at a factory level. Workplace control and such soviet-style democracy could only be achieved and sustained if there was a revolution, an insurrection against the old state power

But the central problem was that while L'Ordine Nuovo and Gramsci exercised a decisive influence in Turin, that was not true elsewhere — and in the other great industrial city of Milan in particular. There the factory councils were set up and controlled by the trade union officials and the Socialist Party, who ensured they were kept free of contamination from Turin. The metal workers' union, FIOM, saw the occupations as merely a means to pressure the Giolitti government into acting as an arbiter between them and the employers.

Gramsci and L'Ordine Nuovo were effectively isolated in Turin. He had argued that Milan was the "fulcrum" of the revolution because "communist revolution in Milan signifies communist revolution in Italy, for in effect Milan is the capital of the bourgeois dictatorship" (Gramsci, SPW 1910-20, p152).

Gramsci argued that taking over the factories was a crucial step but matters had to go further. Crucially the workers had to move on to take over the real centres of capitalist power: the means of communication, the banks, the armed forces and the rest of the state.

The factory owners demanded troops clear the factories but the central government did not have sufficient

soldiers and doubted their loyalty. Instead the government looked to the trade union and Socialist Party
leaders to solve the problem. Despite their revolutionary
rhetoric they were trapped like rabbits in the headlights
at the revolutionary turn of events.

Yet Gramsci did not draw the conclusion that revolutionaries had to break from the PSI to form a separate
Communist Party until the spring of 1920 — when the
revolutionary crisis had already engulfed the Italian left.
For Gramsci and a section of the left in Turin it was, in
the circumstances, relatively easy to make this jump in
short order, but in order to win the majority of the factory councils and the PSI's national membership time
was needed and time was in short supply.

The historian Gwyn Williams comments, "The socialists of Italy, unable to take either the reformist or the
revolutionary road, had no magic left in them. They had
no bluff, except the final one. They responded to their
deepest instincts; they reverted to 'normal'. They put
the issue to the vote" (Gwyn Williams, Proletarian Order,
Pluto, 1975, pp255-256).

The two groups met in Milan. They asked the Turin
delegates if they were ready to launch an armed insurrection. Scared of once more being asked to rise alone
they answered, "No." The trade union leaders then asked
the Socialist Party to make a revolution. They answered,
"No." Finally, in the midst of a revolutionary crisis, they
referred the matter to a trade union congress!

This was not made up of representatives from the
factory councils but from union branches, thus cut-
ting out the most militant workers. Incredibly, the
motion for revolution almost won. But delegates

representing 591,245 voted against, 409,569 voted for, 93,623 abstained, and the resolution to have a revolution failed. The CGL and PSI had their excuse to do nothing sealed in a vote, and the movement was defeated.

The militant rail workers and maritime workers were present but could not vote. Those voting tended to be union loyalists and officials, all of which makes the narrowness of the result even more remarkable. The union leaders then negotiated improved wages and conditions plus promises that the unions would have a say in how the factories were run. With much difficulty they won acceptance of this package and an end to the factory occupations.

For three to four weeks the workers had taken over and run the factories without wages. It was a remarkable achievement. The occupations did not begin to crumble until the PSI and CGL leadership played out their debate about revolution.

Was it a revolutionary moment? No, if the answer depends on the prospects for an immediate launch of a nationwide insurrection. But if we understand revolution as a process in which an alternative power emerges in opposition to the bourgeois state with the potential to eventually supplant it, then this was a revolutionary situation. The factory councils held that possibility, if they could have broken out of Turin. Certainly the violence and extremity of the reaction that followed were a tribute to the scare the employers had undergone.

★ 10: THE BIRTH OF THE COMMUNIST PARTY

After the defeat of the factory occupations one voice stood out on the left with simplistic clarity — that of Amadeo Bordiga. Before everyone else he had called out loudly for a break with the PSI and the creation of a separate Communist Party. After the defeat of the factory occupations he offered the only clear and decisive course of action — making a break which would be far enough to the left to ensure a cohesive and ideologically pure Communist Party. In the autumn of 1920 that seemed good sense to the scattered forces of revolution. Frustration and anger with Serrati's refusal to decisively break with the reformists and with the lack of any clear direction mixed with an abundance of rhetoric fuelled support on the far left for such a course of action.

The trouble was, while Bordiga was right about the need to create a Communist Party, his case for separating and creating a new party was based on a number of other deeply flawed arguments — boycotting elections and urging workers to leave the existing trade unions.

Bordiga had denounced the factory councils and their supporters, L'Ordine Nuovo. He held an elitist view of the party as the self-appointed leadership of the working class taking it by the hand towards liberation. Gramsci always saw a party as an instrument with which workers would themselves achieve revolution. Bordiga saw the party as creating, controlling and directing the factory councils or soviets, reducing them to secondary bodies.

Across Italy the disparate forces of the revolutionary left were coming together to form a Communist Party. But Gramsci was peripheral to this process, with dangerous consequences. His failure to build a national network of supporters sympathising with the ideas of the ordinovisti meant he was left isolated and unable to decisively influence events. He largely abstained from inner party debates, seeing his task as educating the working class. Where Bordiga argued for simply declaring a true Communist Party, Gramsci believed the groundwork for it had to be prepared first at a grassroots level. Gramsci also rejected abstaining from elections, believing they could be used to get across a revolutionary message while parliament could be a platform from which to broadcast real solutions to the country's problems.

Bordiga saw no role for factory councils or soviets in the revolution, only for the party. He even opposed the creation of factory councils before the revolution had succeeded. After the revolution, when soviets were to be set up they were to be based on the local branches of the Communist Party rather than elected in the factories and workshops.

In 1920 Bordiga stressed three things: the need to split the PSI, abstention from bourgeois elections and criticism of the factory councils. He counterposed revolution to participation in parliamentary elections but offered nothing concrete in order to win workers from the latter to the former. A call to abstain did nothing to address those workers who accepted, to whatever degree, the idea that change could come through parliament. Further, for Bordiga, all that was needed was to pass the right resolution or manifesto so that workers would then see the error of their ways.

The majority of Italy's Socialist Party supported the Russian Revolution and the need for revolution. It seemed a certainty that they would rally together in a new, clearly revolutionary party, breaking with those who were loyal to parliamentary democracy.

But this was not to be. Rather than the reformists walking out of the party it was Bordiga and his supporters (including Gramsci) who did so at the PSI's January 1921 congress in Livorno. The new Communist Party that they founded was isolated at birth. Gramsci's instincts were almost always right but his confidence was wrecked by his inability to forge a revolutionary organisation capable of meeting the challenge of the biennio rosso.

Looking back on the divide at the Livorno congress of the PSI and the creation of the Communist Party, Gramsci recalled Lenin saying, "'Separate yourselves from Turati [the right wing leader of the PSI], and then make an alliance with him'… In other words, we should — as our indispensable and historically necessary task — have separated ourselves not just from reformism, but also from the maximalism which in reality represented and still represents the typical Italian opportunism in the workers' movement. But after that, and though continuing the ideological and organisational struggle against them, we should have sought to make an alliance against reaction" (Gramsci, SPW 1921–1926, p380).

Lenin's advice would stay with Gramsci until the end of his life. The question was almost immediately posed in the Italy of 1921.

★ 11: THE FORWARD MARCH OF MUSSOLINI

Antonio Gramsci could see far and clear. At the height of the biennio rosso, in May 1920, he had warned, "The present phase of the class struggle in Italy is the phase that precedes: either the conquest of political power on the part of the revolutionary proletariat...or a tremendous reaction on the part of the propertied class and the governing caste. No violence will be spared in subjecting the industrial and agricultural proletariat to servile labour" (Gramsci, SPW 1910-1920, p191).

His words were not rhetoric. The Italian working class would pay a terrible price for letting the moment of revolution pass when the Fascists took power in October 1922.

The ex-socialist Mussolini had been a fringe figure unable to find a niche until late in 1920. His small grouping, the fascio, was unable to decide whether it was on the left or the right. During the factory occupations Mussolini had wandered round Milan expressing his sympathy for the workers.

But throughout 1921 and 1922 the growing fascist

bands were able to create terror in the countryside and then the towns, burning union offices, socialist newspapers and agricultural co-operatives, and beating and murdering union and left wing activists.

The fascist offensive began in the north eastern border region round Trieste which was contested with Yugoslavia, with fascist bands terrorising Slav communities. It then switched to Bologna and the Po valley. Gangs of ex-officers, students and middle class youth, funded by their liberal fathers and armed by the military, began a campaign of terror against the rural trade unions and socialist-led local authorities.

The left had won control of local councils in these areas and even if they were led by moderate socialists this was sufficient to enrage the landowners who were used to absolute control. Despite their revolutionary rhetoric the PSI were unable to respond to these paramilitary bands. Beginning in Bologna they were chased from council office. Rural trade union clubs were burnt down and activists were beaten and killed.

Mussolini swung in behind these squads and, with some difficulty, made himself leader of a national fascist party. Whole swathes of the countryside passed into fascist control with all workers' organisations of any shade destroyed. The offensive moved on to the smaller towns and cities (fascism never went on the offensive in cities like Turin until it was entrenched in power).

The Italian left was thrown into confusion about how to respond. The right wing of the PSI and the trade union leaders argued that workers and peasants should rely on the forces of law and order to defend them from the fascist menace (despite the fact that the army, police and courts were aiding Mussolini's squads). The maximalists like Serrati simply argued for socialism but offered no strategy for the way forward.

But his opponents on the revolutionary left were little better, arguing that workers had no interest in defending liberal democracy, suggesting that if fascism destroyed parliament that would remove illusions in parliamentary change and insisting there could be no unity with non-revolutionary workers against fascist violence as this would dilute their revolutionary purity.

Never was Gramsci's vision needed more. But he was at his most isolated and confused at the hour of greatest danger.

★12:
RESISTING
FASCISM

In the absence of any national leadership, groups of ex-soldiers and militant workers combined in anti-fascist organisations known as the Arditi del popolo to physically stop the fascists in Rome, Parma, Livorno, Le Spezia and elsewhere. Tragically they found themselves denounced not just by the trade union leaders and the PSI but also by the new Communist Party.

The union leaders and the PSI's leaders even signed a non-violence pact with Mussolini that the Duce ignored but which helped to disarm resistance to fascism. Then they swung over to calling a general strike as fascism seemed to be approaching victory. With little or no preparation the strike collapsed.

Gramsci's instinct was to support the Arditi but he withdrew his backing when the Communist Party leadership decided otherwise. He grasped that fascism would mean the complete destruction of working class organisation and indeed any organisation independent of the state. But like everyone else the Communist Party leaders assumed that if Mussolini took office it would be just another change of government and he would be absorbed into the parliamentary system. Again Gramsci was forced to stay silent and even to repeat some of this rubbish.

The ultra-left attitude of the new party was extended

to the Alliance of Labour, formed to resist fascism, in February 1922, by the CGL, the seafarers' union, together with the anarchist and the syndicalist union federations. Suspicion of the ability of the union leaders to pursue wholehearted resistance to the fascists was one thing but it was another not to try and extend this national initiative into local united resistance. The new party simply did not relate to needs of a working class that understood the mortal danger from fascism. In October 1922 Mussolini took power in Italy. Bordiga played down the significance of the fascist victory.

Fascism was a new phenomenon and anyone could be forgiven for not having a rounded analysis of it or of underestimating its virulence. But Bordiga was profoundly wrong in seeing fascism as just another brand of conventional ruling class politics. Once in power fascist squads would go on the rampage even in Turin. As Mussolini gained strength all opponents and all independent voices would be closed down and all organisations independent of the state or church proscribed.

The strain of publicly supporting the party line that he privately disagreed with threatened Gramsci's health. A way out was found when it was agreed he would be the PCI's representative to the Communist International in Moscow. He arrived at the close of 1922 in time for the Fourth Congress of the Communist International and then the strain of his work, his isolation and the fascist offensive all combined to cause a nervous breakdown. In Russia Gramsci recovered. From Moscow and then his next staging post in Vienna he began to fight for the soul of Italian communism.

★13: GRAMSCI FIGHTS TO RE-ORIENTATE THE PARTY

In 1924 Gramsci argued that fascism was born out of a situation where neither the bourgeoisie nor the working class could act decisively to solve society's crisis. This meant fascism was not simply an Italian phenomenon.

Fascism took over the state in opposition to the old ruling political elite but it did not replace the old ruling class with a new one. The Agnelli family and the others still owned FIAT and the other industrial concerns. Fascism opposed the old forms and much of the traditional ideology of the state — the acceptance of the need for some degree of compromise with the working class. Instead fascism replaced the old policy of consent with the suppression of all forms of working class organisation and any organisations independent of state or church. This marked it off from other forms of ruling class regime.

Gramsci became increasingly frustrated with the way

GRAMSCI *A Rebel's Guide*

that the Italian Communists presented themselves as the self-appointed leadership of the working class. Pointing to a far more dynamic inter-relationship between a party, the working class and mass movements than that offered by Bordiga, he argued, "The party has not been seen as the result of a dialectical process, in which the spontaneous movement of the revolutionary masses and the organising and directing will of the centre converge. It has been seen merely as something suspended in the air; something with its own autonomous and self-generated development; something which the masses will join when the situation is right and the crest of the revolutionary wave is at its highest point..." (SPW 1920-26, p198).

An opportunity to put this sort of politics into practice came with a crisis that threatened to end fascism's rule. In April 1924 the reformist socialist Matteotti delivered a stinging attack on Mussolini in the Italian parliament. The dictator was heard to ask why something was not done about this man. A few days later Matteotti was kidnapped on the streets of Rome and his corpse was later discovered outside the city. The killing was quickly traced to a squad working directly for Mussolini.

The regime tottered, its supporters paralysed. There was widespread anger at the murder and a sense that fascism would be swept away by the crisis. But the various liberal and right wing socialist deputies who criticised the killing limited themselves to walking out of parliament to set up shop elsewhere in Rome. Gramsci called for a united campaign by all anti-fascist parties but one based on mobilisation not gestures, calling for a general strike against the regime.

The Communist Party attempted to develop the spontaneous demonstrations into a more powerful challenge to the regime. Gramsci reported on the party's growth that followed: "Our movement has taken a great step forward: the paper has trebled its circulation, and in many centres our comrades assumed the leadership of the mass movement and attempted to disarm the Fascists, while our slogans were acclaimed and repeated in the motions passed at factory meetings. I believe that our party has become a real mass party in those last few days" (Giuseppe Fiori, Antonio Gramsci: Life of a Revolutionary, Verso, 1990, p174).

For Gramsci too the democrats could not lead the resistance to fascism. His hatred of bourgeois democracy shines through but he understood it was not enough just to "unmask" or denounce bourgeois democracy — the working class and the oppressed had to be won to revolution.

Gramsci's party was an interventionist one. For Bordiga the party would form cadres who would act at the appropriate historic moment. For Gramsci communists were an active and alert part of every movement. The party had to be an integral part of a working class even when it still largely supported social democracy.

Between 1924 and 1926 Gramsci was able to win real control over the party, rearming it and breaking from Bordiga's sectarian approach. In January 1926 Gramsci drew up, along with Palmiro Togliatti, the Lyon Theses, his most mature political document and a guide to the rearming of the party and its conversion into a popular force.

Unfortunately the failure of the opposition to build

on the anger over Matteotti's death allowed Mussolini to draw breath, to regroup and to re-establish an even tighter dictatorship. One of the measures withdrew the protection from prosecution afforded to parliamentary deputies. Gramsci was arrested and jailed. The judge in giving sentence said, "We must stop his brain for working for 20 years." The fascists would fail in that as with much else!

★14: THE PRISON YEARS

Aside from a few happy months when he found himself on an island off Sicily with other communists and anti-fascists, Gramsci's prison term was kept in virtual isolation. As was intended, his health suffered. Afflicted by (among other things) tuberculosis, arterio-sclerosis and Pott's disease (which ate away at his spine) his body gradually disintegrated. His great fear was that his terrible physical condition would lead him to capitulate and plead for special treatment from the regime. He never did.

His incredible will power drove him forward and, despite everything, between 1929 and 1935 Gramsci worked on a series of handwritten notebooks that, against the odds, got out to safety. The Prison Notebooks were written in extraordinarily difficult conditions and with no Marxist classics available (he had to quote these from memory). Gramsci succeeded in filling 2,848 closely packed pages in 33 notebooks.

In 1935 illness prevented Gramsci from writing any more and he was released into the custody of a Rome clinic reflecting the pressure of an international campaign to liberate him and other victims of fascism. But it was too late and he would die in April 1937.

The notebooks were Gramsci's legacy, but they were written in a code to evade the prison censors. So Marxism was termed "the philosophy of praxis" and "the modern prince" was used for the revolutionary party (in homage to the Renaissance writer Machiavelli) and so on. Gramsci's isolation cut him off from the wider debates in the communist movement. This ensured that he escaped the contamination of Stalinism, but crucially it also meant that he could not understand its impact. These two facts allowed those who came after Gramsci to try and appropriate the Prison Notebooks for their own ends.

The Italian Communist Party first published them, selectively, after World War Two. From then on the party used them to justify their strategy of a "long march through the institutions of the Italian state". In other words Gramsci was being used to justify the parliamentary road to socialism he had poured such scorn on. Gramsci's battle for hegemony — popular acceptance of particular ideas — was reduced to winning 51 percent of the vote.

Much later, as the 20th century drew to its close, a generation of postmodernist media studies academics used him, supposedly, to justify their belief that the messenger was the message and that hegemony was about occupying niches in the mass media in order to influence public opinion.

In fact underlying the Prison Notebooks was a fight Gramsci was waging with the leadership of the Italian Communist Party, who were now following directions from Stalin in Moscow. In 1929 Stalin, now increasingly exercising dictatorial power, declared that capitalism faced a final crisis and revolution was the order of the day. Accordingly, the PCI's leadership called for an immediate uprising to overthrow fascism. ·

Gramsci knew this was hogwash, and dangerous hogwash at that. Italy was not on the edge of insurrection. His whole effort at rebuilding the party and re-orientating it on building a united resistance to Mussolini was squandered.

The prison study group Gramsci was involved in at his jail in Puglia broke up when he argued that revolution was not on the immediate agenda and that the task of the hour was for communists to unite with other anti-fascists.

He saw this as a way for the party to intervene and to mobilise the masses while putting forward its own conception of a workers' republic based on workers' and peasants' soviets. He told his brother of his opposition to the new line but his brother decided to withhold this from Togliatti and the party leadership, fearing Gramsci's expulsion.

The Prison Notebooks have to be read in this light. Far from rejecting revolution, Gramsci returned to the argument about how it could be achieved in Western Europe, urging patience as a revolutionary virtue. For Gramsci, armed insurrection was still the "decisive moment of struggle", and his "modern prince" — the revolutionary party — the central, coordinating and generalising body.

★15: REVOLUTION IN THE WEST

In his Prison Notebooks Gramsci asked why the revolutionary upsurge that had swept Western Europe in the wake of the Russian Revolution had failed. Lenin, Trotsky and other Bolshevik leaders had argued that the course of revolution would be more prolonged in the West than in Russia. Now Gramsci returned to that argument and developed it. In doing so, he also deepened Karl Marx's analysis of ideology in important ways.

The difference facing revolutionaries in Western Europe and in Russia was central to the Prison Notebooks. Gramsci argued, "In the East the state was everything, civil society was primordial and gelatinous; in the West, there was a proper relation between state and civil society, and when the state trembled a sturdy structure of civil society was at once revealed" (Gramsci, Selections from Prison Notebooks, p238).

The ruling class was for Gramsci like the mythical centaur, half man, half beast. It ruled both through the use of state coercion and through the consent of those over whom it ruled.

In Tsarist Russia civil society (where social and political life could be organised outside direct state control) was only just emerging. There was little popular acceptance of Tsarist rule and the regime relied directly on repression. This meant, in turn, any crisis tended to grow into a revolutionary confrontation with the state. The task for revolutionaries was to lead a direct assault on power when the opportunity arose. Gramsci called this a "war of manoeuvre".

In Western Europe, on the other hand, the ruling class rested mainly on consent and was able to rely on a variety of institutions within civil society which organised and reinforced this. Gramsci described these as acting like a complicated series of earthworks surrounding a great fortress — the state. So institutions like the church, the media, the education system and political parties helped secure the consent of the masses, allowing force to be used sparingly and only in the last resort. Indeed, far from making the state less of a threat in the West this meant it was stronger than in Russia and would be harder to overthrow.

So these networks of support for the ruling class in civil society and the ideas they helped to reinforce had to be undermined first through a long ideological struggle before a direct assault on the ruling class was possible. This he called a "war of position". Communists had to set themselves the task of undermining the consent, however grudgingly given, which allowed capitalism to rule.

How was that hegemony to be broken down and a rival, revolutionary hegemony achieved?

★16: COMMON SENSE AND GOOD SENSE

Gramsci stressed the need to build alliances in Italy — chiefly between the northern working class and the southern peasantry. But beyond that he was championing the strategy of the united front as presented by Lenin at the Third and Fourth Congresses of the Communist International in the early 1920s.

Sectarian hostility towards building such alliances or united fronts was a consequence of the mechanical approach by Bordiga and his followers in dismissing fascism as simply another form of capitalist rule. Stalin and the Comintern were now repeating this mistake.

Crucial to building such alliances is the development and education of the revolutionary forces through agitation and propaganda. The whole united front approach Gramsci was championing was about working with people with whom you agree on some fundamentals but disagree on others. It is also about addressing the mix of ideas in people's heads, or what Gramsci termed "contradictory consciousness".

Gramsci made an important distinction between

ideas that reflected "common sense" — in reality the ideas of the ruling class — and "good sense", ideas that begin to express the real experience and interests of workers, even if initially it's just a sense of "them and us".

Gramsci explained that popular consciousness contains all sorts of modern and progressive ideas together with some terrible throwbacks. For Gramsci a worker could be a "walking anachronism, a fossil" expressing all sorts of racist and sexist ideas but at the same time a loyal trade unionist who would never cross a picket line. Workers' ideas "contain Stone Age elements and principles of a more advanced science, prejudices from all the past phases of history at the local level and institutions of a future philosophy which will be that of a human race united the world over" (Gramsci, SPN, p324).

Conflicting views of the world can coexist in our minds. Gramsci summed it up this way: "One might almost say he [the worker] has two theoretical consciousnesses (or one contradictory consciousness): one which is implicit in his activity and which really unites him with his fellow workers in the practical transformation of the real world; and one, superficially explicit or verbal, which he has inherited from the past and uncritically absorbed" (Gramsci, SPN, p333).

How can the elements of "good sense" be separated out from "common sense" to foster the development of workers' real class consciousness? How can Marxists develop the positive ideas held by workers into a more coherent critique of the world?

Gramsci insisted this process wasn't something simply imposed from the outside by revolutionaries.

He emphasised that "it is not a question of introducing from scratch a scientific form of thought into everyone's individual life, but of renovating and making 'critical' an already existing activity" (Gramsci, SPN, pp330-331).

He also made the important point that workers often act in ways that contradict what they say. Workers often spontaneously fight back as the underlying conflict between capital and labour comes to the surface, despite espousing the dominant ideology. Out of such battles workers can begin to develop new ideas.

The task for Marxists as Gramsci saw it was to develop the insights thrown up by such battles, the elements of workers' "good sense", into a generalised overall world-view that begins to create a popular collective will to change the world.

Looking back on his own experience of the Turin working class he argued that such spontaneous rebellions of the working class were crucial: "This element of 'spontaneity' was not neglected and even less despised. It was educated, directed, purged of extraneous contaminations" (Gramsci, SPN, p198). Gramsci argued for a unity of "spontaneity" and conscious leadership. This is a dynamic two-way relationship between the revolutionary party and the working class.

So to become effective, class consciousness must be institutionalised. To ensure that the gains of spontaneous struggles are made permanent they must be given organisational expression which allows them to be articulated and strengthened.

★17: PARTIES AND CLASSES

But if Marxists attempt to develop "good sense" into a rounded class consciousness, other forces also attempt to institutionalise workers' contradictory consciousness in ways that prevent this development, or at least to stop it going beyond a certain point. So at times right wing parties have been able to organise some workers around an unalloyed ruling class "common sense". For example, the Tory party in Britain has at points in the past received support from a significant minority of workers.

But the most important expression of workers' contradictory consciousness has been the mass reformist parties. Traditionally as the working class has developed it has adopted a political outlook that looks for justice, equality and change but which also accepts the common sense of political life laid down by the ruling class, that we have to play by parliamentary rules. Here we see a combination of acceptance of ruling class ideas together with their partial rejection, where "common sense" coexists with elements of "good sense" inside large numbers of workers' heads. The result has been the dominance of parties like the Labour Party in Britain, the European socialist parties and the Brazilian Workers Party.

Gramsci also understood that it is not enough for the ruling class to pump out its ideas centrally through the media. Those ideas have to be taken up by people and incorporated into everyday life. In Gramsci's Italy the ruling class relied on teachers, lawyers, priests and journalists to transmit its ideas down into society, to translate them into the language of the mass of the population.

The ruling class still relies on these networks. Thus for over three decades in Britain there has been a constant battle to shift the school curriculum in an ever narrower and conventional direction. But increasingly politicians like Tony Blair look to the media as the prime way to get their message across. But simply relying on the media to convey a message to passive recipients is a potential weakness. There is not an active connection with its supporters that can be used to mobilise them.

When Britain joined the attack on Iraq in 2003 the government tried to pump out a series of lies justifying war. But these simply did not connect. In contrast the anti-war movement began to construct networks across the country that not only gained support for their arguments but also began to mobilise in huge numbers. This in turn created a crisis at the top of society which irrevocably damaged Tony Blair, split New Labour, and led to widespread questioning of how Britain was ruled.

Traditionally Labour or its European sister parties were mass membership parties with activists in every working class community. In one sense they acted as a barrier against some of the most reactionary ideas but at moments of acute struggle they also acted to constrain working class insurgency. Reformism acts both as a shield defending working class interests and as the key blockage preventing any further advance. But today those roots are withering.

This brings us back to the whole relationship between a party, the working class and mass movements, which was at the core of Gramsci's concerns.

Gramsci argued against claims that Marxism provides some sort of crystal ball that allows us to predict the future: "In reality one can 'scientifically' foresee only the struggle, but not the concrete moments of the struggle, which cannot but be the results of opposing forces in continuous movement, which are never reducible to fixed quantities since within them quantity is continually becoming quality. In reality one can 'foresee' to the extent that one acts, to the extent that one applies a voluntary effort and therefore contributes concretely to creating the result 'foreseen'" (Gramsci, Prison Notebooks, p438).

The battle between "good sense" and the old "common sense" is never spontaneously resolved. It is a battle that has to be won. At this point Gramsci argues networks of revolutionaries have to exist which have gathered the confidence of their fellow workers in common struggle, who can put forward a strategy ensuring the new triumphs over the old.

★18: THE GROWING 'ORGANIC CRISIS'

Workers have lived under democracy for over a century in north western Europe and for decades in Germany and southern Europe. They enjoy the right to vote and to organise — as long as that does not entail a direct challenge to the system. They have benefited from welfare reforms, access to education and healthcare, even if these have been rolled back somewhat in recent years, and have not seen a catastrophic fall in their living standards.

Reformism grows out of a situation where trade unions can still at least have a say in how wages are set or workplace conditions are decided. In parliament and the local council chamber reformist parties might promise to deliver some improvements in everyday life or at least act as a dented shield protecting workers from the absolute ravages of the market.

Trade unions separate their economic aims from their political aims. The rule of capital is not challenged in itself. The unions simply demand a place at the negotiating table. The use of economic power to bring political change is ruled out. Meanwhile their twins, the reformist parties, accept the parliamentary system and the norms of the bourgeois state as the confines of their activity.

Both groups accept that this is "their" state to be defended in time of war, it is "their" economy to be defended from unfair foreign competition, and it is "their" judicial system that has to be complied with. For the majority of workers and the oppressed most of the time there is no reason to believe that the system cannot be made to work if the right candidates or parties are elected. The idea that power has to pass to the working class in order to ensure social and economic progress is held by a minority.

Over the last three decades the international capitalist system has experienced a series of great economic crises interspersed with brief periods of boom; globally there has been a shift from a welfare state to a free market or neo-liberal economic and social consensus with disastrous results; the balance of power has also changed beyond recognition with the demise of the USSR, the rise of China and the concerted effort by US imperialism to bolster and assert its hegemony. In Britain there is a specific crisis as the British ruling class tries to stem and reverse Britain's long term decline.

This has led to a crisis at the top of society — an "organic crisis" — creating the terrain on which the "forces of opposition" can organise, as Gramsci put it. The first five years of the 21st century have seen a growing resistance to a global neo-liberal agenda, and a global anti-war movement on a scale never seen before. In several countries, including Britain, we have also seen radical left formations emerge to contest the pro-market left on the parliamentary terrain. So far the economic struggle has lagged behind because of the defeats workers took in the 1980s and 1990s but there are indications of how that could shift.

In this situation many of Gramsci's arguments — about the nature of reformism and how workers can be won to revolutionary ideas — take on a new and fresh vitality.

★19: WORKERS, DEMOCRACY AND REVOLUTION

Gramsci's focus on workers might seem irrelevant to those who accept the idea that the working class is a shrinking force in today's world. But globally it is growing and now, for the first time, embraces the majority of the world's population. Conditions in cities like Sao Paolo or Shanghai approximate to those in Gramsci's Turin. In Western Europe the vast majority either work, study to work or are retired from work. Great factories still produce vast profits (and if their workforce is smaller it gives them a greater hold over the production process). But many of us work in call centres, the finance sector, hypermarkets, distribution, and other generally low paid and precarious jobs.

In Britain people came together in their millions in their opposition to the Afghan and Iraq wars of 2002 and 2003 and the subsequent occupations. They recognised common concerns. But because the struggle has not exploded to the same extent in the workplace there is not the same sense of class identity and power.

In that sense the situation is not so different from Turin after World War One, where a new workforce crowded into an expanding city. Then the existing

institutions of the working class were not up to mobil-
ising and organising them. Gramsci saw the factory
councils as key to the creation of a new working class
force.

Factory (or better, workplace) councils have been
thrown up, at least in embryo, in every great revolutionary struggle of the century that followed the 1905 Russian
Revolution. In May and June 2005 a revolutionary insurrection swept Bolivia with popular assemblies taking
control of working class communities, toppling a neo-
liberal government attempting to sell off the country's
oil and gas resources.

In everyday capitalist democracy, formally everyone
has one vote and we are all equal. But this is not the true
reality. Rupert Murdoch and the governor of the Bank
of England exercise power in a way the vast majority of
us never will. There is a vast division between political
and economic power, leaving us with just a very limited say over what happens in society, say 20 percent,
but excluding ordinary people from the slightest control over the other 80 percent, the economy or market.
Workplace councils break down the barriers separating
political and economic power. People meet and decide
as citizens, producers and consumers.

Our electoral system also divides us into geographical constituencies that mask the fact that the key divide
is between classes and not geographical areas and that
in each of these areas there is no "natural" community
but huge divisions of wealth. Workplace council democracy brings people together on the basis of the activity
that dominates their lives — their relationship to work
and exploitation.

When we elect MPs or councillors we have no control over them. In a factory council system all representatives can be questioned and voted out. Furthermore they are rank and file representatives enjoying the same wage as those they represent — not two or three times more. Parliamentary democracy does its best to exclude people from involvement. Too often we are encouraged to see politics as boring — which in terms of the House of Commons, it is. Often we have no say whatsoever over the police, army, media, civil service, judges and so on.

Workplace council democracy maximises involvement and destroys the alienation of ordinary people from the decision-making process. It gives people a sense of what they are capable of and shows that we can run things. It is vital in shrugging off the crap of ages whereby we are led to believe we are incapable of controlling our lives.

Rank and file movements have repeatedly sprung up in opposition to trade union officialdom. Whether or not they can develop a stage further into workplace councils depends on the level of struggle and the level of generalisation in the working class. Revolutionaries cannot call that up through an act of will but they can develop rank and file movements in preparation for a situation where the tradition they have established can blossom out into workplace councils.

For revolutionaries there is not an option of waiting for that moment. The lesson from Italy's biennio rosso was that a revolutionary force had to exist in advance of that moment: an interventionist force active in the daily struggles of workers — in other words a party. This revolutionary force had to relate to the mass of workers who accept reformist ideas but who can be influenced through the struggle for immediate day to day demands, and thus at a moment of crisis be won to a revolutionary conclusion. Revolutionaries have to be beside these workers in their unions, but working all the time to counter the hold of trade union leaders and reformist politicians who would use their influence to blunt and contain a revolutionary thrust.

Gramsci once observed that at moments of crisis people gather in rival parties even if they refuse to use that name or reject the idea of parties in the abstract. In other words, people gather round particular strategies — ultimately those of reform or revolution. But as we have seen the two sides are not equal. Behind one stands all the "common sense" which we have soaked in since birth, reinforced by the Labour Party, the trade union leaders and all sorts of siren voices. To take a leap into a new society requires overcoming all this. Revolutions might begin spontaneously but they never end so.

Gramsci understood that workplace councils were not simply planned and neither were they simply spontaneous. Both elements had to merge together in a dynamic way. For him, one role of such councils was to act as a bridge between the minority organised in the revolutionary party and the great mass of workers who still to some degree accept reformist ideas.

On its own a party is too small to move those millions. Thirty or 40 years ago in Britain there existed a powerful network of shop stewards elected directly in the workplace and prepared to take action independently of their union officials. Socialists saw the possibility of organising them into a powerful rank and file movement, with the potential to be a bridge to the mass of workers, and laying the basis for workers' councils.

Today the radicalisation around war, imperialism and neo-liberalism is outpacing the economic struggle but a new generation of revolutionaries need to address how they can give identity to a workforce that exists but has yet to rediscover its power.

Gramsci is a powerful ally in achieving that — and much more.

NOTE ON READING

Extensive material from Gramsci's prison notebooks has been published by Lawrence and Wishart as Antonio Gramsci, Selections from Prison Notebooks (1971). The same publisher has also produced two volumes of Gramsci's main writings from the biennio rosso and the rise of Fascism – Selections From Political Writings 1910-1920 (1977) and Selections From Political Writings 1921-1926 (1978).

A number of Gramsci's articles are also available from the Marxist Internet Archive: http://www.marxists.org.uk/archive/gramsci/index.htm

The best biography of Grasmci is Giuseppe Fiori, Antonio Gramsci: Life of a Revolutionary (Verso, 1990). For a look at Fascism's road to power see Tom Behan, The Resistible Rise of Benito Mussolini (Bookmarks, 2002).

Also available in the Rebel Guide Series...

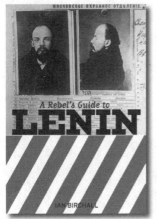

Pick up your copies now from Bookmarks, Britain's leading socialist bookshop. Just around the corner from the TUC and the British Museum. We stock a huge range of books: classic and contemporary Marxism, anti-war and anti-capitalism, trade union resources and British labour history, radical fiction, culture and an excellent children's section. We have DVDs, audio CDs and political journals together with a well stocked second hand section and much more...

We also do a full mail order service
Bookmarks, 1 Bloomsbury Street, London WC1B 3QE
www.bookmarks.uk.com
020 7637 1848